CAMBRIDGE PRIMARY
Science

Skills Builder

6

Fiona Baxter and Liz Dilley

CAMBRIDGE
UNIVERSITY PRESS

CAMBRIDGE
UNIVERSITY PRESS

University Printing House, Cambridge CB2 8BS, United Kingdom

Cambridge University Press is part of the University of Cambridge.

It furthers the University's mission by disseminating knowledge in the pursuit of education, learning and research at the highest international levels of excellence.

Information on this title: education.cambridge.org

© Cambridge University Press 2016

First published 2016

Produced for Cambridge University Press by
White-Thomson Publishing
www.wtpub.co.uk

Editor: Sonya Newland
Designer: Clare Nicholas

Printed in Poland by Opolgraf

A catalogue record for this publication is available from the British Library

ISBN 978-1-316-61109-8 Paperback

Additional resources for this publication at www.cambridge.org/

Cover artwork: Bill Bolton

....

Contents

Introduction

This series of primary science activity books complements *Cambridge Primary Science* and promotes, through practice, learner confidence and depth of knowledge in the skills of scientific enquiry (SE) and key scientific vocabulary and concepts. These activity books will:

- enhance and extend learners' scientific knowledge and facts
- promote scientific enquiry skills and learning in order to think like a scientist
- advance each learner's knowledge and use of scientific vocabulary and concepts in their correct context.

The *Skills Builders* activity books consolidate core topics that learners have *already* covered in the classroom, providing those learners with that extra reinforcement of SE skills, vocabulary topic knowledge and understanding. They have been written with a focus on scientific literacy with ESL/EAL learners in mind.

How to use the activity books

These activity books have been designed for use by individual learners, either in the classroom or at home. As teachers and as parents, you can decide how and when they are used by your learner to best improve their progress. The *Skills Builder* activity books target specific topics (lessons) from Grades 1–6 from all the units covered in *Cambridge Primary Science*. This targeted approach has been carefully designed to consolidate topics where it is most needed.

How to use the units

Unit introduction

Each unit starts with an introduction for you as the teacher or parent. It clearly sets out which topics are covered in the unit and the learning objectives of the activities in each section. This is where you can work with learners to select all, most or just one of the sections according to individual needs.

The introduction also provides advice and tips on how best to support the learner in the skills of scientific enquiry and in the practice of key scientific vocabulary.

Sections

Each section matches a corresponding lesson in the main series. Sections contain write-in activities that are supported by:

- Key words – key vocabulary for the topic, also highlighted in bold in the sections
- Key facts – a short fact to support the activities where relevant
- Look and learn – where needed, activities are supported with scientific exemplars for extra support of how to treat a concept or scientific method
- Remember – tips for the learner to steer them in the right direction.

How to approach the write-in activities

Teachers and parents are advised to provide students with a blank A5 notebook at the start of each grade for learners to use alongside these activity books. Most activities will provide enough space for the answers required. However, some learner responses – especially to enquiry-type questions – may require more space for notes. Keeping notes and plans models how scientists work and encourages learners to explore and record their thinking, leaving the activity books for the final, more focused answers.

Think about it questions

Each unit also contains some questions for discussion at home with parents, or at school. Although learners will record the outcomes of their discussions in the activity book, these questions are intended to encourage the students to think more deeply.

Self-assessment

Each section in the unit ends with a self-assessment opportunity for learners: empty circles with short learning statements. Teachers or parents can ask learners to complete the circles in a number of ways, depending on their age and preference, e.g. with faces, traffic light colours or numbers. The completed self-assessments provide teachers with a clearer understanding of how best to progress and support individual learners.

Glossary of key words and concepts

At the end of each activity book there is a glossary of key scientific words and concepts arranged by unit. Learners are regularly reminded to practise saying these words out loud and in sentences to improve communication skills in scientific literacy.

1 Humans and animals

What learners will practise and reinforce

The activities in this Skills Builder unit give learners further practice in the following topics in the Learner's Book and Activity Book:

Topic	In this topic, learners will:
1.1 Body organs	identify organs in the body
1.2 The heart	explain how the heart works
1.4 The lungs and breathing	complete sentences about the lungs and breathing
1.5 The digestive system	see Challenge, Section 1.5
1.6 What do the kidneys do?	investigate factors that affect kidney function
1.7 What does the brain do?	see Challenge, Section 1.7

Help your learner

In this unit, learners will practise using a table to present results and using results to draw conclusions and make predictions (Section 1.6). To help them:

1 Remind learners to use a ruler when drawing the rows and columns of a table. They should also draw a border around it. Each column should have a heading and units. The factor that will change should be in the left-hand column. The factors to be observed or measured should be on the right.

2 Talk about each of the organs and their functions in the body. Ask learners to point out where each organ is found in their body.

TEACHING TIP

Remind learners that a prediction is something you think will happen based on what you already know or have observed.

LOOK AND LEARN

The different **organs** of the body work together to help you survive. The heart and lungs work together to make sure all parts of your body get **oxygen**. The liver breaks down harmful substances so that the kidneys can remove them. The liver produces substances that help the body **digest** food.

Identify the organs of the body

Look at the diagram. The organs have the wrong labels. Write the correct name for each organ in the space next to the incorrect label.

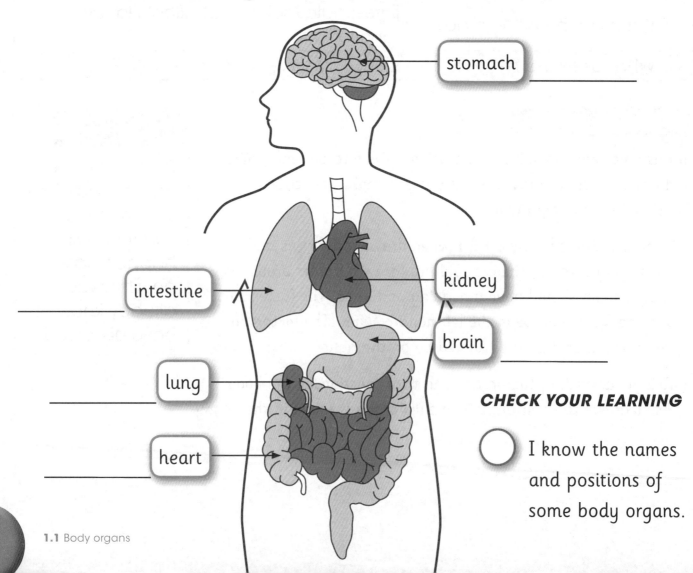

CHECK YOUR LEARNING

○ I know the names and positions of some body organs.

1.2 The heart

KEY FACT

The **heart** is a muscle that never rests. It **contracts** about 72 times every minute to keep pumping blood around the body. The blood carries food and oxygen to all parts of the body.

Explain the way the heart works

Circle the letter of the correct answer to the following questions about the heart.

1 The heart pumps blood that ...

    a contains oxygen only

    b contains carbon dioxide only

    c contains both oxygen and carbon dioxide.

2 The heart pumps blood to ...

    a all parts of the body

    b the lungs only

    c the kidneys only.

Complete sentences about the lungs and breathing

1 Use the words in the box to complete the sentences.

| blood | ribs | **lungs** | **windpipe** | nose | carbon dioxide | oxygen |

We **breathe** in air through our _____.

The air we breathe in contains _____.

The air moves down the _____ and into

our _____. The air then moves into the

_____. We breathe out air that contains

_____. The _____

protect our breathing system.

2 **Think about it!**

There is less oxygen in the air in very high places, such as in the Andes or Himalaya Mountains. How do people who live in those places get enough oxygen?

_____

_____

CHECK YOUR LEARNING

○ I know about the lungs and breathing.

○ I know which gases we breathe in and breathe out.

○ I can find out how people who live in very high places get enough oxygen.

volume, urine, factors,
conclusion, prediction

Investigate how the kidneys work

Miguel kept a record of the weather and what he did for five days.

Monday – very hot day, played soccer all afternoon, drank 300 ml of water
Tuesday – cool day, drank 2 litres of water
Wednesday – fairly hot, drank 1 litre of water, walked to friend's house
Thursday – cold day, drank 5 cups of tea
Friday – very hot day, drank no water, played soccer all afternoon

The bar chart shows the volume of urine he produced each day.

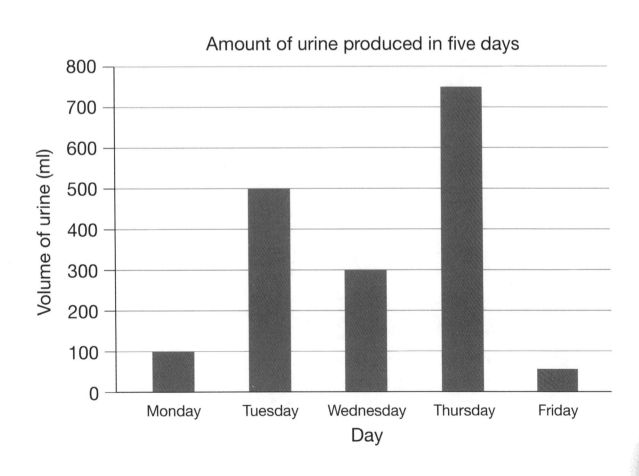

Amount of urine produced in five days

1 **Use the information in the bar chart to create a table.**

2 On which day did Miguel produce:

a most urine?

_____

b least urine?

_____

3 a How many millilitres of urine did he produce on Tuesday?

_____

b Why do you think he produced this much urine on Tuesday?

_____

_____

_____

4 Use the results to write a **conclusion** about the factors that affect how much urine Miguel produced.

_____

_____

_____

_____

5 Predict how many millilitres of urine Miguel would produce on Saturday if it was a fairly hot day and he drank 1 litre of water while he did his homework. Add your **prediction** to the table. Explain your prediction.

_____

_____

_____

_____

CHECK YOUR LEARNING

◯ I can present results in a table.

◯ I can obtain information from a graph.

◯ I can use results to draw a conclusion and make a prediction.

2 Living things in the environment

What learners will practise and reinforce

The activities in this Skills Builder unit give learners further practice in the following topics in the Learner's Book and Activity Book:

Topic	In this topic, learners will:
2.1 Food chains in a local habitat	observe a tree habitat
2.2 Food chains begin with plants	answer questions about how pot plants make food
2.3 Consumers in food chains	identify consumers, predators and prey and draw food chains
2.4 Food chains in different habitats	identify food chains in a tropical forest habitat
2.5 Deforestation	see Challenge, Section 2.5
2.6 Air pollution	see Challenge, Section 2.6
2.7 Acid rain	see Challenge, Section 2.7
2.8 Recycling	investigate the effects of recycling
2.9 Take care of your environment	identify positive and negative effects on the environment

Help your learner

In this unit, learners will practise making relevant observations (Sections 2.1 and 2.3). They will also make predictions using scientific knowledge and understanding (Sections 2.3 and 2.4). To help them:

1 Talk about pot plants you have at home and the way you look after them.

2 Look at the packaging of food at home and in the supermarket, and discuss it with learners. Talk about which types of packaging can be recycled.

TEACHING TIP

Encourage learners to watch nature programmes on TV to practise identifying the producers, consumers, predators and prey.

2.1 Food chains in a local habitat

Observe a tree habitat

Resources

You will need a tree, a pair of binoculars, reference books on birds and insects.

1 Identify the tree you have chosen.

_____

2 Does the tree have leaves or flowers or fruits?

_____

3 **a** Name all the animals you can see eating the leaves or flowers or fruits.

_____

_____

_____

b Draw a **food chain** to show the feeding relationship between one of these animals and the tree.

_____

Remember:

Food chains describe the feeding relationship between plants and animals.

4 **a** Look on the ground by the roots of the tree. Look for insects in the dried leaves and seeds. Name the insects you find.

_____

_____

_____

b Draw a food chain to show the feeding relationship between one of these insects and the tree.

_____

Remember:

When you draw a food chain, the arrow must go from the food to the animal eating the food.

5 Why is the tree called a **habitat** for the animals you have named?

_____

_____

_____

CHECK YOUR LEARNING

○ I can identify feeding relationships in a tree.

○ I can draw a food chain.

2.2 Food chains begin with plants

producers, consumer

Identify the things that pot plants need to stay alive

Ploy likes to cook. She does not have a garden but she grows herbs in pots. She has Thai basil, lemon grass and chilli in pots on the windowsill.

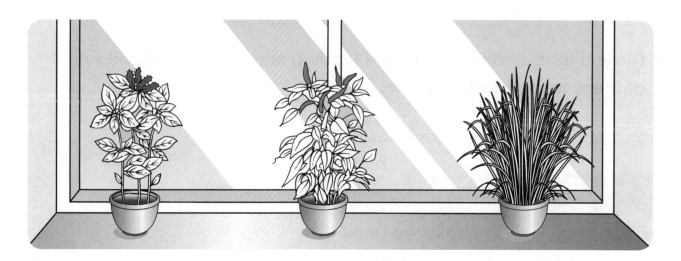

1 Why do we call plants **producers?**

_____

_____

2 List the three things that plants need to make food.

_____

_____

3 Why does Ploy keep her pot plants on the windowsill?

_____

_____

4 Why does Ploy water her pot plants every day?

_____

_____

5 One day Ploy finds holes in some of the leaves of her Thai basil plant. She sees a caterpillar on her plant.

a What do we call an animal that eats a plant?

_____

b Draw a food chain to show the feeding relationship between the caterpillar and the Thai basil. Label the producer and the **consumer**.

> **Remember:**
> A food chain must always begin with a producer.

_____

6 Think about it!

Explain how Ploy gets energy from the herbs she has grown when she eats them.

_____

_____

_____

CHECK YOUR LEARNING

◯ I know what plants need to make food.

◯ I can draw a food chain showing a producer and a consumer.

LOOK AND LEARN

In every habitat, there are plants and animals. Animals are consumers because they eat plants or animals to get their energy. Some animals only eat plants. Many animals eat other animals. An animal that eats another animal is called a **predator**. The animal that a predator eats is called its **prey**.

Identify consumers, predators and prey

Look at the pictures below.

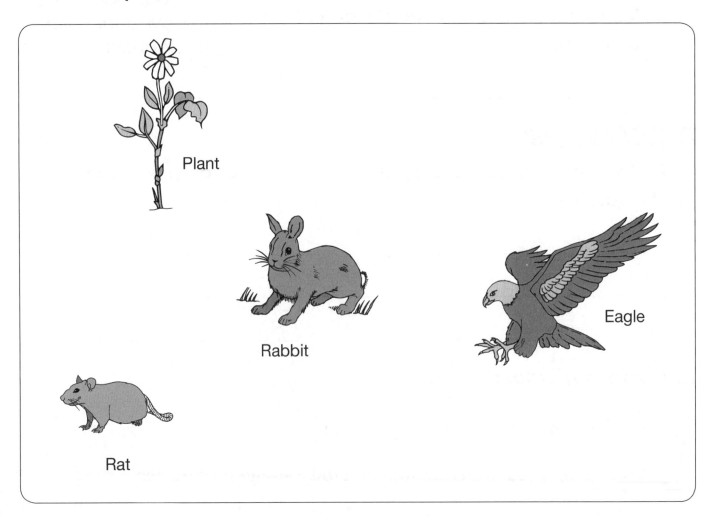

Plant

Rabbit

Eagle

Rat

1 Name the two consumers that only eat plants.

_____

_____

2 Which animal is the predator?

_____

3 Which animals are prey for this predator?

_____

_____

4 Draw a food chain for a producer and a consumer from the picture.

_____

5 Draw a food chain for a producer, a predator and prey from the picture.

_____

6 Think about it!

Think of another animal that could be prey for the predator in the picture.

_____

CHECK YOUR LEARNING

◯ I know the difference between consumers, predators and prey.

◯ I can show feeding relationships in food chains.

canopy

Identify food chains in a tropical forest habitat

Look at the diagram of a tropical forest habitat.

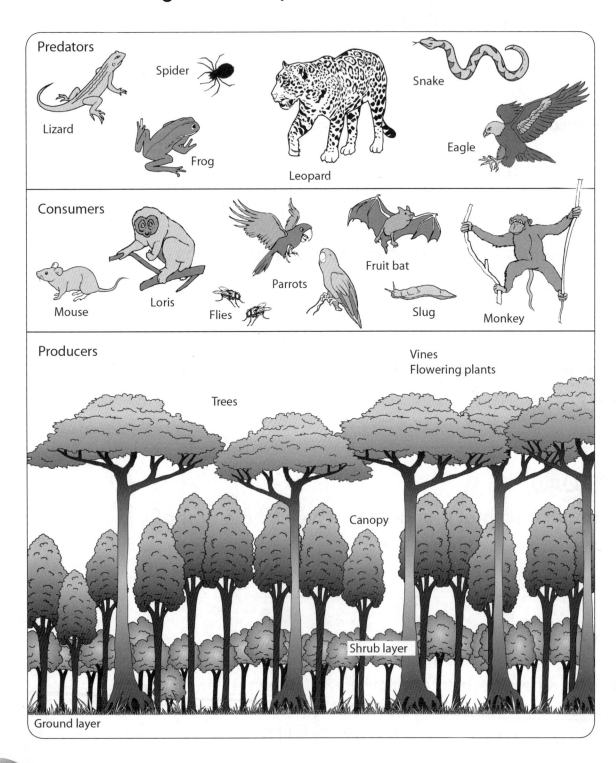

1 a List the types of producers in the tropical forest.

_____

_____

_____

b What types of food do consumers get from these producers?

_____

_____

_____

2 Draw three food chains between a producer and a consumer, using examples from the diagram.

_____

_____

_____

KEY FACT

Tropical forests grow in very hot, wet areas. The trees grow to different heights. The tallest trees grow to about 50 m and form a **canopy** that stops sunlight reaching the lower levels. Some animals live on the shady forest floor and others live in the trees.

3 Rewrite this food chain in the correct order.

slug ⟶ leaves ⟶ lizard

_____

4 Draw another three food chains between a producer, a consumer and a predator, using examples from the picture.

_____

_____

_____

5 **Think about it!**

What negative effect are humans having on the tropical forest habitat? Why is this happening?

_____

_____

_____

_____

CHECK YOUR LEARNING

◯ I can use information from a diagram to draw food chains.

2.8 Recycling

packaging, recycled

How does recycling help the environment?

Mrs Davis has just been to the supermarket. She is packing her shopping away.

KEY FACT

Glass is made from sand. When glass is recycled it is melted down and made into a new glass object. This saves having to dig more sand from the ground. It uses less energy than making new glass.

1 Complete the table to show the materials that the **packaging** for each item is made from and whether it can be **recycled**.

Food item	Packaging is made from	Can packaging be recycled?
rice		
cooking oil		
soy sauce		
lemonade		
fresh chicken		
spinach		

2 Choose one of the types of packaging you said could be recycled. What natural product are we saving by recycling this packaging?

_____

3 a How does recycling glass bottles reduce the amount of waste we produce?

_____

_____

b How does recycling glass bottles reduce the amount of energy we use?

_____

_____

4 a Imagine Mrs Davis gets rid of the packaging by dropping it on the ground outside her home. What is this practice called?

_____

b Why does it have a negative effect on the environment?

_____

_____

CHECK YOUR LEARNING

◯ I can select packaging that can be recycled.

◯ I know that recycling has many positive effects on the environment.

◯ I know that littering has a negative effect on the environment.

2.9 Take care of your environment

Identify good and bad effects on the environment

Look at the pictures in the boxes below. They show some different ways that people affect the **environment**.

1 Draw a cross on the pictures that show *negative effects* on the environment. Fill in the gaps in the sentences beneath these boxes. Choose words from the box.

2 Draw a tick on the pictures that show a way of *caring* for the environment. Fill in the gaps in the sentences beneath these boxes. Choose the words from the box below.

rinse	holes	shower	pollute	germs	litter	waste	less	buses	save

  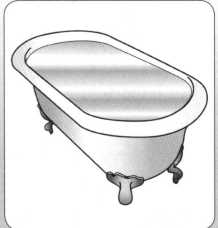

1 Put your _____ in the bin.

2 Flies leave _____ which can make you sick. Keep food and eating areas clean.

3 Use _____ water in the bath. If possible _____ instead.

4 _____ water
– turn on the tap
only when you need
to _____
your teeth.

5 Walking or
cycling does not
_____ the
environment like cars
or _____.

6 Check that your
hosepipe does not
have _____
along the pipe which
will _____
water.

It is important for everyone to play a part in caring for the
environment. There are many different ways of doing this. You
can conserve water and use less energy. You can reduce waste by
recycling packaging and putting food waste on the compost heap.
Encourage your friends and family to do all these things, too.

CHECK YOUR LEARNING

◯ I can identify and describe how to take care of the environment.

3 Material changes

What learners will practise and reinforce

The activities in this Skills Builder unit give learners further practice in the following topics in the Learner's Book and Activity Book:

Topic	In this topic, learners will:
3.1 Reversible and irreversible changes	decide whether changes are reversible or irreversible and explain why
3.2 Mixing and separating solids	see Challenge, Section 3.2
3.3 Soluble and insoluble substances	identify soluble and insoluble solids
3.4 Separating insoluble substances	separate oil and water
3.5 Solutions	see Challenge, Section 3.5
3.6 How can we make solids dissolve faster?	draw a graph of results and identify factors that affect dissolving
3.7 Grain size and dissolving	see Challenge, Section 3.7

Help your learner

In this unit, learners will practise presenting results in a line graph and identifying patterns in results (Section 3.6). They will also use results to draw conclusions (Sections 3.4 and 3.6), make predictions using scientific knowledge (Sections 3.1 and 3.4) and make observations using simple apparatus correctly (Section 3.4). To help them:

1 Explain that there can be different patterns in results. Sometimes we see the pattern as we change the factor we are investigating. For example sugar dissolves faster as we increase the water temperature. Another pattern might be that some results are the same. For example the bulb in a circuit lights up when there is a metal object in the circuit.

reversible, irreversible

Identify and explain reversible and irreversible changes

This is a solid gold bar. When you heat the bar it melts.

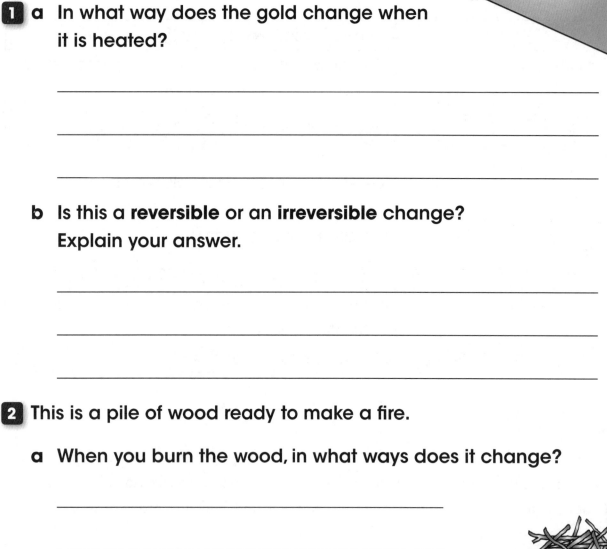

1 **a** In what way does the gold change when it is heated?

_____

_____

_____

b Is this a **reversible** or an **irreversible** change? Explain your answer.

_____

_____

_____

2 This is a pile of wood ready to make a fire.

a When you burn the wood, in what ways does it change?

_____

_____

_____

b Is this a reversible or an irreversible change?
Explain your answer.

_____

_____

_____

3 Mrs Mulia puts this carton of orange juice in her freezer.

a In what ways does the juice change when she puts
it in the freezer?

_____

_____

_____

b Is this a reversible or an irreversible change?
Explain your answer.

_____

_____

_____

CHECK YOUR LEARNING

I can use scientific knowledge to identify and explain reversible and
irreversible changes.

dissolve, soluble, insoluble, mixtures

LOOK AND LEARN

Substances that **dissolve** in liquids are **soluble**. They mix completely with the liquid, so you cannot see them once they have dissolved, but they are still present in the solution. Substances that do not dissolve in liquids are **insoluble**. They do not mix with the liquid – they form a suspension.

Identify mixtures with soluble and insoluble solids

Magda investigated dissolving. She mixed three different solids with water. The pictures show her results.

A

B

C

1 Are the solids soluble or insoluble in water?

A is _____

B is _____

C is _____

2 a Name two ways that you know if a solid is soluble.

_____

_____

b What is a **mixture** of a liquid and a soluble solid called?

_____

3 a Name two ways that you know if a solid is insoluble.

_____

_____

b What is a mixture of a liquid and an insoluble solid called?

_____

4 Think about it!

Magda's little brother thought there was water in Beaker C.
He drank some and quickly spat it out. He said it was salty.
Explain why this happened.

_____

_____

CHECK YOUR LEARNING

◯ I can identify soluble and insoluble solids and give reasons.

◯ I can name mixtures of a liquid and soluble and insoluble solids.

◯ I understand that a dissolved substance is still present in a solution.

Make a filter to separate oil and water

Resources
You will need a clear plastic bottle with a lid, a basin, some sticky putty, water and cooking oil.

Have you heard the expression 'Oil and water don't mix'? You are going to prove that this is true.

To make a **filter**:

- Make a hole in the bottom of the plastic bottle.
- Push sticky putty into the hole.
- Pour any quantity of oil and water into the bottle.
- Put the lid on the bottle and shake it well to mix the oil and water.

1 Is the oil soluble or insoluble in water? Explain why you know.

_____

_____

_____

_____

KEY FACT

Filtering can be used to separate soluble and insoluble substances. Filters work by letting soluble substances pass through tiny holes. The larger particles in insoluble substances cannot get through the holes.

2 Leave the bottle to stand for five minutes. Draw a picture of what you see in the bottle after five minutes. Label your drawing.

3 Describe a way in which you could get the oil and water back into two separate containers using your apparatus.

_____

_____

_____

4 Complete this sentence to write a **conclusion** about what you have discovered:

I can _____ oil and water using a

_____ because oil is _____

in water.

5 **Think about it!**

Why do you need to use water and washing-up liquid to clean oil off a pan?

_____

_____

_____

_____

CHECK YOUR LEARNING

◯ I can make and use a filter to separate oil and water.

◯ I can explain my results and write a conclusion using my scientific knowledge.

LOOK AND LEARN

If you leave a solute in a solvent for a long enough time, the solute will dissolve. This is because the particles in liquid substances are constantly moving. Any **factor** that makes the liquid solvent particles move faster or brings more solute particles into contact with the solvent will make the solute dissolve faster.

Identify factors that affect dissolving

Maya investigated the factors that affect the speed at which sugar dissolves in water. She recorded her results in a table.

Number of stirs	Time sugar took dissolve (minutes)
0	30
1	28
2	25
3	20
4	21
5	10

KEY FACT

A solution is the product of a soluble substance dissolving in a liquid. There are always two parts to a solution: the solute (the substance that dissolves) and the solvent (the liquid in which the solute dissolves).

1 Draw a graph of Maya's results.

2 a Which factor did Maya investigate?

_____

b Name another factor that affects the speed at which sugar dissolves.

_____

3 a Describe the pattern you can see in the results.

_____

_____

b Which result does not fit the pattern? Explain why.

_____

_____

_____

4 Maya decided to check this result. Describe a way she could do this. Why will this help her?

_____

_____

_____

5 Does the factor Maya investigated affect dissolving? Write a conclusion for the investigation.

_____

_____

Remember:

A conclusion is what you find out in an investigation. Your conclusion should always be related to the aim of the investigation. For example if you tried to find out which materials conduct electricity, then your conclusion should state which of the materials you tested conduct electricity.

CHECK YOUR LEARNING

○ I can draw a graph of results.

○ I can recognise a pattern in results and identify results that do not fit the pattern.

○ I can use results to draw a conclusion.

4 Forces and motion

What learners will practise and reinforce

The activities in this Skills Builder unit give learners further practice in the following topics in the Learner's Book and Activity Book:

Topic	In this topic, learners will:
4.1 Mass and weight	investigate mass and weight
4.2 How forces act	identify the forces acting on a bicycle
4.3 Balanced and unbalanced forces	see Challenge, Section 4.3
4.4 The effects of forces	identify the effects of forces on objects
4.5 Forces and energy	see Challenge, Section 4.5
4.6 Friction	explain why friction is useful
4.7 Investigating friction	see Challenge, Section 4.7
4.8 Air resistance and drag	investigate and explain how air resistance affects falling objects

Help your learner

In this unit, learners will practise making relevant observations using simple apparatus correctly and collecting evidence to test a prediction (Section 4.8). To help them:

1 Remind learners to drop the pieces of paper from the same height at the same time when they are investigating air resistance.

2 When making predictions, help learners by discussing their initial observations and explanations, and showing them how this can lead to accurate predictions.

TEACHING TIP

Demonstrate how the nature of a surface affects friction by letting learners roll a marble across different surfaces, such as a carpet, tiled floor and newspaper.

mass, weight, kilograms, newtons, forcemeter, gravity

Understand mass and weight

1 Read these statements about **mass** and **weight**.

Mark each of the statements as true (✓) or false (✗).

forcemeter

☐ **a** Mass and weight are the same.

☐ **b** We measure mass in **kilograms**.

☐ **c** We measure weight in **newtons**.

☐ **d** Weight is the amount of matter in an object.

☐ **e** The reading on the **forcemeter** is 30 newtons.

Remember:

The force of **gravity** pulls objects towards the Earth. Weight is the amount of force caused by gravity acting on an object.

3 Think about it!

Mr Large has mass of 90 kg on earth. On planet Zogg, the force of gravity is only half as strong as it is on Earth. What will Mr Large's weight be on planet Zogg? Explain your answer.

_____

_____

_____

CHECK YOUR LEARNING

○ I can identify true and false statements about mass and weight.

LOOK AND LEARN

Forces always act in pairs that work in opposite directions. If you are holding an object in the air, you are exerting an upward force on it, but the object is also exerting a downward force. If the forces are the same size, they are said to be balanced. If one force is bigger than the other, they are said to be unbalanced. When forces are balanced, an object will remain stationary. If forces are unbalanced, an object will move in the direction of the force.

Identify the forces acting on a bicycle

Look at the picture of the boy on the bicycle.

1 **a** Draw arrows on the picture to show the direction of the forces acting on the bicycle.

b Name two ways that forces act as shown by the arrows you have drawn.

_____

_____

2 When will the forces acting on the bicycle be equal?

_____

3 Which force must be bigger in order for the bicycle to move forward? Tick the correct answer.

☐ The force acting on the wheels.

☐ The forces acting on the pedals.

> ### Remember:
>
> The downward force on an object is caused by gravity pulling it down.

CHECK YOUR LEARNING

◯ I can label a picture to show the forces acting on a bicycle.

◯ I know when the forces on a bicycle are equal.

◯ I know which force must be bigger for a bicycle to move.

Identify the effects of forces on objects

1 In each of the following examples, identify the effect of the force on the object. Choose from:

- Makes an object move.
- Changes the direction of a moving object.
- Changes the shape of an object.
- Changes the speed of an object.

a Gita pedals her bicycle faster.

b Emma cracks an egg into a bowl.

c Magda pushes open a door.

d Giorgio hits a tennis ball back to Mark.

_____

e Ali chews a piece of apple.

_____

KEY FACT

Forces can speed up the movement of objects, such as when you exert a force to make a ball roll across a surface. Forces also slow objects down or stop them, such as if you catch a ball.

2 Use the words in the box to complete these sentences about energy in movement. You will use one of the words more than once.

> transfer   move   energy

a Forces make objects _____.

b We give an object _____ when we exert a force on it.

c Moving objects have _____.

d Forces _____ energy to objects to make them move.

> **Remember:**
>
> When we exert a force on an object to make it move, we are transferring energy to that object. The amount of energy transferred is called work.

CHECK YOUR LEARNING

◯ I can explain the effects of forces on objects.

◯ I understand how forces are linked to energy and movement.

Explain why friction is useful

1 Read these sentences about **friction**. Underline the correct words to complete the sentences.

   a Friction is caused when two surfaces *rub/stick* together.

   b Friction *can/cannot* make an object move.

   c Friction *speeds up/slows down* moving objects.

   d Friction changes *heat/movement* energy into *heat/movement* energy.

   e Friction helps objects *slide/grip* on surfaces.

KEY FACT

Friction is a force that slows down movement between surfaces. In liquids, friction is called drag. Although liquids slow down objects moving through them, they also make surfaces smoother and reduce friction between two solids rubbing together.

Remember:

The force of friction is greater between rough surfaces than it is between smooth surfaces.

2 Is it better to wear trainers or ballet shoes if you are walking on a smooth, polished floor? Explain your answer.

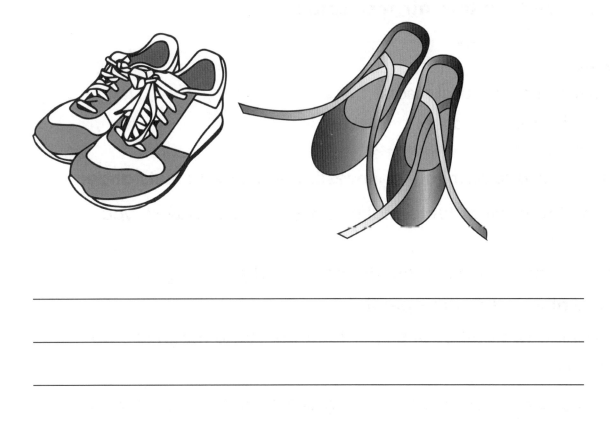

_____

_____

_____

_____

KEY FACT

Friction can be useful, but it can also be a problem. The heat caused by friction as objects rub against one another can cause them to wear out. This is why the soles of your shoes wear down and car tyres must be replaced from time to time.

CHECK YOUR LEARNING

◯ I can complete sentences about friction.

◯ I can explain why friction is useful.

4.8 Air resistance and drag

Investigate and explain air resistance

Resources
You will need three identical pieces of paper and a chair or table.

Follow these steps to carry out an investigation into air resistance:

- Stand on the chair or table. Make sure you are steady so you don't fall off.
- Hold one piece of paper with the narrow edge facing down.
- Hold the other piece of paper flat.
- Let go of the two pieces of paper from the same height at the same time.

1 Which piece of paper reaches the ground first? Use what you know about forces to explain why.

_____

_____

_____

_____

KEY FACT

Air resistance is also called 'drag'. The larger the surface area of the moving object, the greater the air resistance will be.

Be careful when standing on a chair or table. Make sure it is on a flat surface. Wear shoes with a good grip so you do not slide off.

2 **a** Predict whether a piece of paper folded in four would drop faster or slower than a flat, unfolded piece of paper. Explain your prediction.

_____

_____

_____

_____

b Test your prediction. Were you correct?

_____

_____

3 **a** In which direction does air resistance act on falling objects?

_____

b Name the force that acts in the opposite direction to air resistance on falling objects.

_____

CHECK YOUR LEARNING

◯ I can explain the way air resistance acts on falling objects.

◯ I can use scientific knowledge to make and explain a prediction.

Electrical conductors and insulators

5

The activities in this Skills Builder unit give learners further practice in the following topics in the Learner's Book and Activity Book:

Topic	In this topic, learners will:
5.1 Which materials conduct electricity?	discover which materials conduct electricity
5.2 Does water conduct electricity?	see Challenge, Section 5.2
5.3 Do different metals conduct electricity equally well?	see Challenge, Section 5.3
5.4 Choosing the right materials for electrical appliances	observe why certain materials are used to make an electric plug
5.5 Circuit symbols	recognise the components of a circuit by their symbols
5.6 Changing the number of components	understand what happens when you change the number of bulbs and cells in a circuit
5.7 Adding different components	predict whether or not different components will work in a circuit
5.8 Length and thickness of wire in a circuit	see Challenge, Section 5.8
5.9 How scientists invented batteries	see Challenge, Section 5.9

Help your learner

In this unit, learners will practise making predictions using scientific knowledge and understanding (Sections 5.1, 5.4 and 5.7), collecting evidence and data to test predictions, and saying whether evidence supports predictions, and using results to draw conclusions and make further predictions (Section 5.1). They will also practise presenting results in tables (Section 5.1) and representing series circuits with conventional symbols (Sections 5.5 and 5.7). To help them:

1 Ask questions such as 'What do you think will happen now?' (to practise prediction) and 'Was that what you thought would happen?' (to practise testing whether evidence supports predictions).

2 Help learners with the practical work in 5.1 by providing the resources and guiding them if necessary.

TEACHING TIP

Most of the activities in this section will need to be done at school using the apparatus available there, under the supervision of a teacher.

conductor, insulator

Test which materials conduct electricity

> **Resources**
> You will need a 1.5 V cell, a 1.5 V bulb in a bulb holder, three pieces of 15 cm
> connecting wire, a coin, a wooden chopstick, a glass and a plastic cup.

1 Predict which of the following objects will conduct electricity
and which will not. Put a tick (✓) next to the objects that will
conduct electricity and a cross (✗) next to the ones that won't.

- [ ] the coin
- [ ] the chopstick
- [ ] the glass
- [ ] the plastic cup.

Connect the circuit with the cell, the bulb in the bulb holder and
three lengths of wire as shown below. Scrape one centimetre of
plastic off the two loose ends of connecting wire.

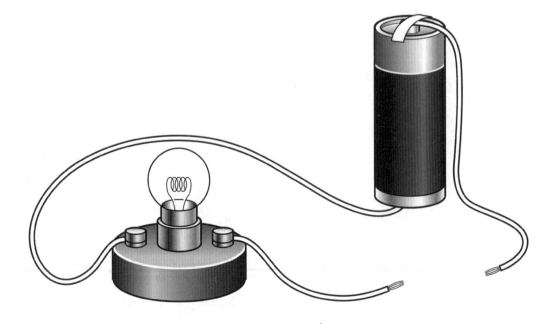

Test that your circuit works. Holding the plastic coated wires, allow the bare metal wires to touch each other. Does the bulb light up? If not, check each of the connections you made and test again.

Now test each object by holding one of the plastic coated wires in each hand so that the bare wires touch each end of the object. Observe the bulb to see if it lights up. If the bulb lights up, the object conducts electricity. If the bulb does not light up, the object does not conduct electricity.

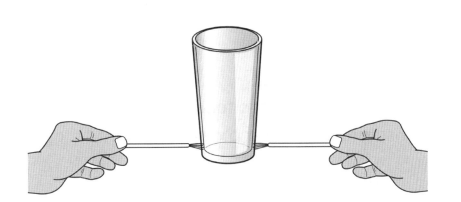

⚠ Always be careful when handling electrical wire – make sure you only handle the plastic coating. Never touch the bare wire.

2 Did the results of the test support your predictions?

_____

3 Use your results to decide whether each object is an electrical **conductor** or an electrical **insulator**. Record your answers in the table.

Object	Material object is made from	Electrical conductor	Electrical insulator

4 Write a conclusion by filling in the blanks in these sentences using the words in the box.

> glass   wood   metal   plastic

_____ objects are electrical conductors. Objects made

from _____, _____ and _____ are

electrical insulators.

5 **Think about it!**

Use your conclusion to explain why you think the following objects will be conductors or insulators: a key, a brass ornament, a plastic bag, a glass bottle.

_____

_____

_____

_____

CHECK YOUR LEARNING

◯ I can use scientific knowledge to predict which objects conduct electricity.

◯ I can collect evidence to test my predictions.

◯ I can use a table to present my results.

◯ I can use my results to draw conclusions and make further predictions.

5.4 Choosing the right materials for electrical appliances

appliances, plug, wall socket

Identify conductors and insulators in a plug

> **LOOK AND LEARN**
>
> **Appliances** such as electrical kettles and electric tools use 110V or 220V. This electricity is strong. To make appliances safe to use, the parts that you touch must be made of materials that are electrical insulators. The parts that electricity passes through must be made of electrical conductors.

1 Write the labels 'conductor' or 'insulator' in the correct spaces on the diagrams below.

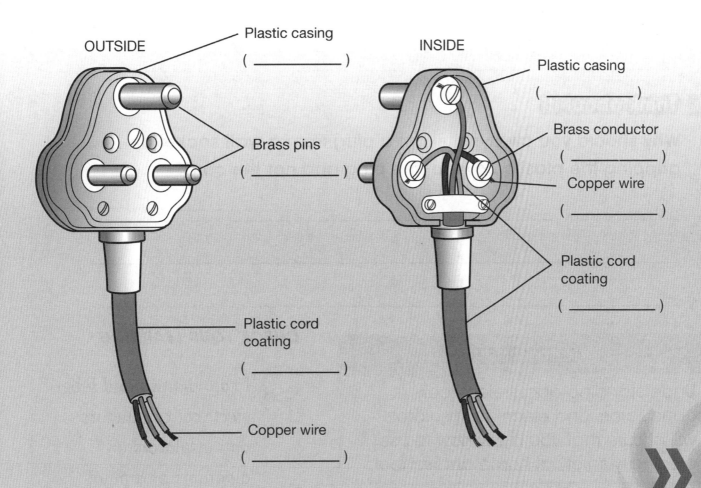

OUTSIDE

Plastic casing
(_____)

Brass pins
(_____)

Plastic cord coating
(_____)

Copper wire
(_____)

INSIDE

Plastic casing
(_____)

Brass conductor
(_____)

Copper wire
(_____)

Plastic cord coating
(_____)

2 Draw the outside of a **plug** or an electrical appliance at home. Label the parts. Write 'conductor' or 'insulator' after each label.

3 Think about it!

Why should you always pull out a plug from a **wall socket** by gripping the plastic cover of the plug and not the cord?

_____

_____

_____

Remember:

Understanding about electrical conductors and electrical insulators will ensure that you know how to use electricity safely at home and school.

CHECK YOUR LEARNING

○ I can identify and label electrical conductors and insulators on diagrams of a plug.

Recognise and use circuit symbols

1 Look at **circuit diagrams** A, B and C.

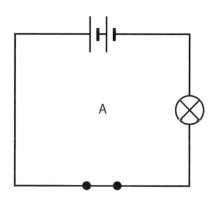 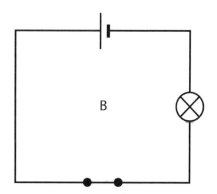 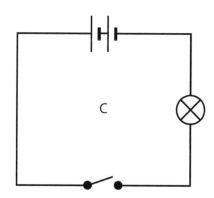

a Which circuit contains one 1.5V cell?

_____

b Which circuit is broken? Explain why.

_____

_____

c In which circuit will the bulb glow brighter? Explain why.

_____

_____

_____

2 Draw a **complete circuit** with two 1.5V cells, two bulbs and a closed switch.

3 Draw a circuit with a bell, four 1.5V cells and an open switch.

CHECK YOUR LEARNING

○ I can recognise circuit **symbols**.

○ I can draw circuit diagram with different components.

Make predictions about components in circuits

Aanjay has made this circuit:

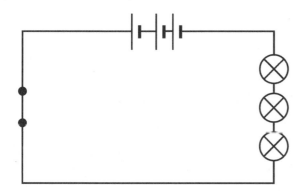

1 **a** List the components in the circuit.

_____

_____

_____

b Will the bulbs light up? Explain your answer.

_____

_____

2 **a** If Aanjay removes a bulb from the circuit, will the remaining two bulbs glow more or less brightly?

_____

b If Aanjay adds a bulb to the circuit, will the bulbs will glow more or less brightly?

_____

3 a If Aanjay removes a cell from the circuit, will the bulbs will glow more or less brightly?

_____

b If Aanjay adds a cell to the circuit, will the bulbs will glow more or less brightly?

_____

4 Use your predictions from Questions 2 and 3 to choose the right words to complete this conclusion:

When you add a bulb to a circuit, all the bulbs will glow _more / less_ brightly than before.

When you remove a bulb from a circuit, all the bulbs will glow _more / less_ brightly than before.

When you add a cell to a circuit, all the bulbs will glow _more / less_ brightly than before.

When you remove a cell from a circuit, all the bulbs will glow _more / less_ brightly than before.

CHECK YOUR LEARNING

◯ I can make predictions about what will happen if you change the number of bulbs or cells in a circuit.

KEY FACT

Different components need different strengths of electricity to work in a circuit. For example if you put a 1.5 V bulb in a circuit, you need one 1.5 V cell for it to work.

Make different components work in circuits

1 Complete the table below. Draw the symbols for the components in the second column.

Component	Symbol	Number of 1.5 V cells needed
buzzer		2
bell		4
motor		16

2 Look at this circuit diagram.

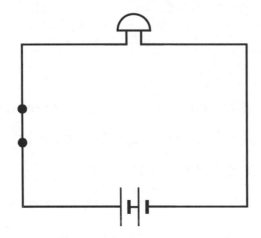

a Will the **bell** ring in this circuit? Explain why or why not.

_____

_____

b How would you change the circuit to make the bell ring?

_____

3 Draw a circuit with a **buzzer**. Remember to supply enough 1.5 V cells to the circuit.

CHECK YOUR LEARNING

○ I can choose the correct number of 1.5 V cells for a component to work in a circuit.

○ I can read and draw circuit diagrams.

5.7 Adding different components

Answers

1 Humans and animals

1.1

Identify the organs of the body

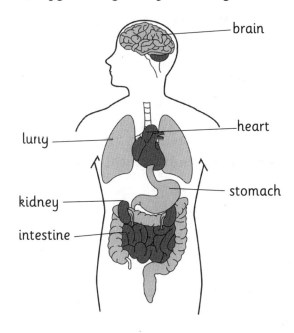

- brain
- heart
- lung
- stomach
- kidney
- intestine

1.2

Explain the way the heart works

1 **a** contains oxygen only.

2 **a** all parts of the body.

1.4

Complete sentences about the lungs and breathing

1 We breathe in air through our <u>nose</u>. The air we breathe in contains <u>oxygen</u>. The air moves down the <u>windpipe</u> and into our <u>lungs</u>. The air then moves into the <u>blood</u>. We breathe out air that contains <u>carbon dioxide</u>. The <u>ribs</u> protect our breathing system.

2 **Think about it!**

The blood carries oxygen in the body in the red blood cells. People who live in very high places have more red blood cells so that they can carry enough oxygen.

1.6

Investigate how the kidneys work

1

Day	Amount/volume of urine produced (ml)
Monday	100
Tuesday	500
Wednesday	300
Thursday	750
Friday	50
Saturday	+- 400 [volume should be less than Tuesday but more than Wednesday]

2 **a** Thursday.

   b Friday.

3 **a** 500 ml.

   b It was cool and he did not play soccer so he did not sweat much; he also drank a lot of water.

4 The amount of water Miguel drank, the temperature/weather and how active he was affected the amount of urine Miguel produced.

5 **Think about it!**

The amount of urine Miguel produced would be less than Tuesday, when he drank 2 litres of water and the day was cool, but more than Wednesday, when he drank the same amount but did more exercise.

2 Living things in the environment

2.1

Observe a tree habitat

1 Learner's own response.

2 Learner's own response.

3 **a** Learner's own response.

   b Food chain must begin with the tree and end with the animal.

4 **a** Learner's own response.

   b Food chain must begin with the tree and end with the animal.

5 It is called a habitat because it provides a home for the animals – they find food and shelter there.

2.2

Identify the things that pot plants need to stay alive

1 Plants are producers because they make their own food.

2 Sunlight, water and carbon dioxide.

3 The Sun shines through the window onto her plants. Without light, plants will die.

4 Plants need water to make food. Without water, plants will die.

5 **a** A consumer.

   b Thai basil (producer) $\rightarrow$ caterpillar (consumer).

6 **Think about it!**
   The herbs make food in the form of sugar. When the family eat the herbs they absorb the sugar and their bodies change the sugar into energy.

2.3

Identify consumers, predators and prey

1 Rabbit and rat.

2 Eagle.

3 Rabbit and rat.

4 Plant $\rightarrow$ rabbit or plant $\rightarrow$ rat.

5 Plant $\rightarrow$ rabbit $\rightarrow$ eagle or

   plant $\rightarrow$ rat $\rightarrow$ eagle.

6 **Think about it!**
   A snake; smaller birds.

2.4

Identify food chains in a tropical forest habitat

1 **a** Trees, vines and flowering plants.

   b Leaves, twigs, seeds, fruits and flowers.

2 fruit $\rightarrow$ fruit bat

   fruit and leaves $\rightarrow$ monkey

   fruit and seeds $\rightarrow$ parrot

   dead leaves $\rightarrow$ fly.

3 leaves $\rightarrow$ slug $\rightarrow$ lizard.

4 seeds $\rightarrow$ mouse $\rightarrow$ snake

   leaves $\rightarrow$ slug $\rightarrow$ frog

   dead leaf $\rightarrow$ fly $\rightarrow$ spider

   seeds $\rightarrow$ mouse $\rightarrow$ eagle.

5 **Think about it!**
   Deforestation. Causes of deforestation are that people want land to grow crops on, they sell the trees for their wood, or the land is used for commercial plantations, especially palm oil.

2.8

How does recycling help the environment?

1

Food item	Packaging is made from	Can packaging be recycled?
rice	cardboard	yes
cooking oil	plastic	Maybe, depending on types of plastic
soy sauce	glass	yes
lemonade	aluminium	yes
fresh chicken	polystyrene/plastic	no
spinach	plastic	no

2 Cardboard – saves trees from being cut down.
Glass – saves sand from being dug out of the earth.
Aluminium – saves aluminium from being mined.

3 a We reuse the glass instead of making new glass.

   b Melting down old glass bottles uses less energy than making new glass.

4 a Littering.

   b It is unsightly; it smells; it attracts flies, which is a health hazard; you can cut yourself on broken glass.

2.9

Identify good and bad effects on the environment

1 Boxes 2, 3, 4 and 6 must have a cross.

2 Boxes 1 and 5 must have a tick.

Sentences under boxes:

1 Put your <u>litter</u> in the bin.

2 Flies leave <u>germs</u> which can make you sick. Keep food and eating areas clean.

3 Use <u>less</u> water in the bath. If possible <u>shower</u> instead.

4 <u>Save</u> water – turn on the tap only when you need to <u>rinse</u> your teeth.

5 Walking or cycling does not <u>pollute</u> the environment like cars or <u>buses</u>.

6 Check that your hosepipe does not have <u>holes</u> along the pipe which will <u>waste</u> water.

3 Material changes

3.1

Identify and explain reversible and irreversible changes

1 a It changes from a solid to a liquid.

   b It is a reversible change because when the liquid gold cools down it will become solid again.

2 a The wood changes into ash.

   b It is an irreversible change because ash will not change back into wood.

3 a The juice changes from a liquid to a solid.

   b It is a reversible change because the juice will become a liquid again when it melts.

3.3

Identify mixtures with soluble and insoluble solids

1 A is insoluble.

   B is insoluble.

   C is soluble.

2 a There are no solids visible in the container. The mixture is clear.

   b A solution.

3 a The liquid is cloudy. Solids settle at the bottom of the container.

   b A suspension.

4 **Think about it!**
He could not see the salt in the solution because it had dissolved. However, the salt was still there, so the liquid tasted salty.

3.4

Make a filter to separate oil and water

1 Oil is insoluble in water. You can see blobs of oil in the water.

2 The drawing should show the bottle with a layer of water on the bottom and a layer of oil on top.

3 You could drain the water into the basin and put the stopper back in the hole when only oil is left so that the oil will stay in the bottle.

4 I can <u>separate</u> oil and water using a <u>filter</u> because oil is <u>insoluble</u> in water.

5 Think about it!
The oil on the pan does not dissolve in water but it does dissolve in washing-up liquid.

3.6

Identify factors that affect dissolving

1
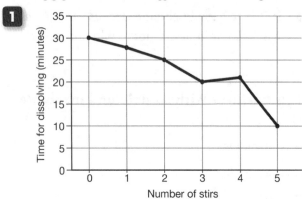

Number of stirs

2 a Stirring.

b Temperature.

3 a The time taken for the sugar to dissolve decreases with more stirs.

b The result for four stirs does not fit. The time taken for dissolving increased.

4 Maya can repeat the investigation. This will help her determine if she got the measurement wrong the first time.

5 Yes. The more times you stir a solution, the faster sugar dissolves.

4 Forces and motion

4.1

Understand mass and weight

1 a Mass and weight are the same. ✗

b We measure mass in kilograms. ✓

c We measure weight in newtons. ✓

d Weight is the amount of matter in an object. ✗

e The reading on the forcemeter is 30 newtons. ✗

2 Think about it!
On Earth Mr Large will weigh 900 N. If the force of gravity on planet Zogg is half that of Earth, he will weigh 450 N.

4.2

Identify the forces acting on a bicycle

1 a

b Forces act in pairs. Forces act in opposite directions.

2 When the bicycle is not moving.

3 The force acting on the pedals.

4.4

Identify the effects of forces on objects

1 a Changes the speed of an object.

b Changes the shape of an object.

c Makes an object move.

d Changes the direction of a moving object.

e Changes the shape of an object.

2 **a** Forces make objects <u>move</u>.

b We give an object <u>energy</u> when we exert a force on it.

c Moving objects have <u>energy</u>.

d Forces <u>transfer</u> energy to objects to make them move.

4.6

Explain why friction is useful

1 **a** Friction is caused when two surfaces <u>rub</u> together.

b Friction <u>cannot</u> make object move.

c Friction <u>slows down</u> moving objects.

d Friction changes <u>movement</u> energy into <u>heat</u> energy.

e Friction helps objects <u>grip</u> on surfaces.

2 Trainers. Friction makes the trainers grip the floor better than the ballet shoes because they have a rougher sole. This will stop you slipping on a smooth polished floor.

4.8

Investigate and explain air resistance

1 The piece of paper with the edge facing down reaches the ground first. It has a smaller surface area for air to push against as it falls. This gives it less air resistance than the piece of paper that was dropped flat.

2 **a** The prediction should be that the folded piece of paper will drop faster than a flat, unfolded piece of paper. The folded piece of paper has a smaller surface area for air resistance to act on.

b Both pieces of paper should be dropped with the flat surface facing down.

3 **a** Upwards.

b Gravity.

5 Electrical conductors and insulators

5.1

Test which materials conduct electricity

1 Correct prediction: the coin will conduct electricity. The chopstick, the glass and the cup will not conduct electricity.

2 Learner's own response.

3

Object	Material object is made from	Electrical conductor	Electrical insulator
coin	metal	✓	
chopstick	wood		✓
glass	glass		✓
cup	plastic		✓

4 <u>Metal</u> objects are electrical conductors. Objects made from <u>wood</u>, <u>glass</u> and <u>plastic</u> are electrical insulators.

5 **Think about it!**
key = conductor
brass ornament = conductor
plastic bag = insulator
glass bottle = insulator.

5.4

Identify conductors and insulators in a plug

1 On the diagram of the outside of the plug, learner must label brass pins and copper wire as conductors, and plastic casing and plastic cord coating as insulators. On the diagram of the inside of the plug, learner must label brass conductor and copper wire as conductors and plastic casing and plastic cord coating as insulators.

2 All plastic coverings are insulators. Any metal parts are conductors.

3 Think about it!

If you pull the cord you could pull it out of the plug casing and expose the bare copper wire. If you touch the bare wire with wet hands with the power switched on, you could get an electric shock.

5.5

Recognise and use circuit symbols

1 a B.

 b C, because the switch is open.

 c A, because it has two cells.

2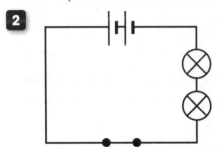

3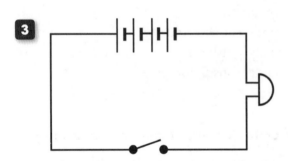

5.6

Make predictions about components in circuits

1 a 3 x 1.5 V cells, 3 bulbs, a switch and wire.

 b Yes. There are enough cells and the switch is closed.

2 a More brightly.

 b Less brightly.

3 a Less brightly.

 b More brightly.

4 When you add a bulb to a circuit, all the bulbs will glow <u>less</u> brightly than before.

When you remove a bulb from a circuit, all the bulbs will glow <u>more</u> brightly than before.

When you add a cell to a circuit, all the bulbs will glow <u>more</u> brightly than before.

When you remove a cell from a circuit, all the bulbs will glow <u>less</u> brightly than before.

5.7

Make different components work in circuits

1

Component	Symbol	Number of 1.5V cells needed
buzzer		2
bell		4
motor		16

2 a No, because it only has two 1.5 V cells and it needs four.

 b Add another two 1.5 V cells to the circuit.

3

Glossary

1 Humans and animals

breathe	the way we take air into our bodies and let it out of our bodies
contracts	when a muscle becomes shorter
conclusion	what you decide is true after looking at results and evidence
digest	to break down food in the body into very tiny particles
factors	items to consider when dealing with a problem or investigation
heart	a special muscle that pumps blood around the body
lungs	the organs we use for breathing
organs	parts inside the body that carry out specific functions to keep us alive
oxygen	a gas that the body needs to stay alive
prediction	something you think will happen based on your observations and scientific knowledge
urine	the liquid waste excreted by the kidneys
volume	the amount of a liquid
windpipe	the tube that carries air from the nose and mouth to the lungs and back

2 Living things in the environment

canopy	the top layer of branches of trees in a forest
consumer	a living thing (usually an animal) that eats plants or another animal
environment	our natural surroundings
food chain	a way to describe the feeding relationship between plants and animals
habitat	the home of a plant or an animal
packaging	material used to wrap something, such as a box or bag
predator	a consumer that eats other animals (which are their prey)
prey	an animal that is eaten by another animal (a predator)
producer	a plant that produces energy from sunlight
recycled	re-processed and made into a new product

3 Material changes

conclusion	what you decide is true after looking at results and evidence
dissolve	when a solid mixes with a liquid and becomes part of the liquid
factor	something to consider when dealing with a problem or investigation
filter	a sieve that lets through liquids and dissolved substances but not insoluble substances
insoluble	cannot dissolve
irreversible	cannot be changed back to what it was before
mixtures	form when two or more different substances are mixed together but are not chemically joined
reversible	can be changed back to what it was before
soluble	can dissolve

4 Forces and motion

air resistance	the force caused by air pushing against moving objects
forcemeter	an instrument used to measure weight and other forces
forces	pushes or pulls that try to change the shape or position of an object
friction	a force between two objects that tries to stop them sliding past each other
gravity	the force that pulls objects towards the Earth
kilograms	the units for measuring mass
mass	the amount of matter in an object, measured in kilograms
newtons	the units for measuring force
weight	the amount of force that pulls an object towards the Earth

5 Electrical conductors and insulators

appliances	useful tools or utensils that use electricity to work
bell	a component that makes a ringing noise when electricity passes through it in a circuit
buzzer	a component that makes a buzzing noise when electricity passes through it in a circuit
circuit diagrams	pictures of a circuit that use symbols to represent components
complete circuit	a circuit with a closed switch, allowing electricity to flow all around it
conductor	a material that allows electricity to pass through it
insulator	a material that does not allow electricity to pass through it

plug	a device for connecting an electrical wire or cable to an electricity supply
symbols	drawings used to represent components in a circuit
wall socket	the plate on the wall where a plug fits

Remember:

Use these words when you discuss the topics in the unit so that learners become familiar with them.